RESCUE OUR HEALTHCARE

By David Reis D.O., F.A.C.E.P.

Copyright 2015

Healthcare costs are out of control. Worse than the cost acceleration is the deterioration of our healthcare quality and services. The underlying cause is medical liability in all its forms, from medical malpractice to product liability to class action suits. The lawyers and lawyer legislators have made a feeding trough out of healthcare. The portrayed benefit by lawyers to the public has been far surpassed by the detriment caused by medical liability on healthcare costs and declining services to the public. The author of this book is a board certified emergency medicine doctor and has practiced full time emergency medicine for 36 years. He is a Fellow of the American College of Emergency Physicians and has been an Assistant Clinical Professor teaching clerks, interns, and residents emergency medicine skills over these years. The author of this book will give the public incite to the deplorable conditions we are facing in our healthcare delivery if a dramatic change in our healthcare laws are not enacted. He will depict the changes that will protect the public, reduce our healthcare costs and improve healthcare services citing decades of experiences in the emergency rooms dealing with these issues. Visit his blog at www.rescueourhealthcare.com for comments and join his "Get Healthcare Out of the Courts Campaign".

PROLOGUE: *Would you enter a career that makes you personally responsible for the well-being of priceless items (humans) whose natural course is deterioration and death to the extent that this career responsibility threatens the loss of all of your own personal assets from medical liability and this career environment significantly threatens your own health and well-being?*

Contents

RESCUE OUR HEALTHCARE

Chapter 1

STATISTICS

Healthcare costs are out of control. We spent 2.9 trillion on healthcare in 2013 which is 17.4% of our total Gross Domestic Product (GDP) in the United States according to the Center for Medicare and Medicaid Services and this is expected to grow to 19.6% by 2024. That is $9,255 per person in 2013. This is also double the cost per person in the average developed European country and double the percent of GDP for the average developed European nation. I believe we have the best medical capability and care in the world that is under threat of serious decline due primarily to our legal system. We have the best research and medical product development and medical treatment systems in the world fostered by our highly competitive system. We have the most Nobel prizes in medicine. We have the best equipped hospitals and advanced technology available to local communities throughout our country. We have the most advanced training programs, medical schools and universities in the world. The wealthy individuals in most countries with a health issue choose to come to the US for their medical care if that is any perceived quality indicator.

Many would argue that our healthcare is inferior to most other developed nations and use statistics like the higher costs, shorter life expectancy and increased infant mortality statistics to conclude this as evidence. I would argue that we in the US are victims of our own success in that we have become technology savvy and sedentary due to our wealth of resources and our pervasive leisurely lifestyles. This has given us the highest obesity rate in the world among developed countries. More than 30% of Americans are obese, defined as having a Body Mass Index (BMI) of 30 or above.

That alone could explain our minimally reduced mortality age and higher infant mortality rate. Another contributor to these adverse statistics is our cost payment structure for our population which is insurance based. Those with good insurance get the best of our medical care and the indigent are denied good preventive care by our primary physicians. The indigent and many poor insurance holders are forced to seek interventional care by going to emergency rooms or urgent care centers. This leaves a significant portion of our population with very poor preventive healthcare. In that sense we fall short of access to our best of medical care.

That said, I do believe we are experiencing a serious decline in the quality of our advanced healthcare especially emergency medical care. I blame this on our legal profession and our litigious society as I shall explain in the ensuing chapters.

The elevated cost structure in the USA compared to the rest of the world as depicted above has one significant aspect unique to the US. The underlying cause of this is our overwhelming cost of Liability, Liability and Liability!!!

We are the most litigious society in the world by far. We have 3-4 times the amount of malpractice suits of any other advanced country in the world and much larger awards than any other country. Class action suits against drugs, medical procedures and other medical products are epidemic in the US and are unethical or illegal in other developed countries. The amount of money siphoned out of healthcare and into law firms is staggering in the US.

We are even witnessing the breakdown of ethics in America. Our children and society have been conditioned that someone else is always responsible for any adversity that they have suffered and that someone deserves to be sued.

Lawyers now advertise and offer a no cost contingency fee structure to clients promoting lawsuits. These both are considered unethical in other developed countries. Class action suits have become rampant with the addition of the ability for professionals to advertise here in the US. Drugs and medical products and procedures have become favorite targets of these class action suits. These class action suits are also illegal in other developed nations.

Although the impact of our litigious society can be extrapolated across all the businesses in America to varying degrees, my focus is going to be about how this relates to the accelerating and uncontrollable costs of healthcare and particularly its adverse impact on emergency medicine, which is my background. It should not surprise anyone that we rank so poorly in quality, availability and cost compared to other developed nations with the unique litigation burden on our healthcare system.

Chapter 2

MEDICAL MALPRACTICE LIABILITY

Medical malpractice insurance costs are the most obvious and quantifiable cost added to our healthcare and these insurance costs are outrageous. The actual insurance awards alone are estimated to be 10 billion dollars according to a Harvard public health study in 2010. This and other studies have trivialized the actual cost impact on medical care in this country as being only a few percent of our total healthcare costs. This minimalizing of liability's impact on our costs for healthcare is laughable to me. This does not include all the product liability for virtually everything used in medical care. This does not include the cost for all of the burdensome documentation processes invented to help us defend ourselves in a lawsuit. This does not consider the complex billing department operations for all the complicated deceitful insurance contracts designed to hide the cost increases from the public. This does not include all the salaries of the growing numbers of hospital attorneys and administrators required on all the hospitals across the country to ensure compliance with federal rules and to institute programs of quality assurance designed to avoid penalties and reduce litigation. This does not include the time and energy extracted from the healthcare workers involved in this litigation. (More about these many additional healthcare cost impacts from medical liability in subsequent chapters).

When I began emergency medicine full-time work back in the late 70s, I had to pay $35,000 dollars yearly for $200/600 thousand malpractice liability policy. This means that I would be covered for defensive costs and a maximum of $200,000 award for any given malpractice suit and a maximum of only 3 of these per year. Now, how comfortable does anyone think a practitioner of emergency medicine should feel with this kind of expensive liability costs for this trivial coverage for the risky work that we are engaged in the emergency rooms across the USA? Very uncomfortable…! Therefore, I began my practice of defensive medicine, doing far more tests and procedures to have documentation and expensive oversight from consults from every venue I could draw upon within reason.

Chapter 3

DEFENSIVE MEDICINE

Defensive medicine is another large factor in the rising costs of healthcare but is difficult to quantify. These are unnecessary tests and procedures done by physicians that are easily justified as documentation and to make more certain a diagnosis and treatment plan is correct given the threatening nature of litigation for failing to diagnose and properly treat or refer patients. This was estimated to be 45.6 billion dollars by the same 2010 Harvard study as above. I'm not sure how they made that estimate but we in the US do twice as many tests and procedures as other developed countries that do not have our liability onus. Therefore, maybe we could cut out half of our costs for our tests and procedures if we could shed this medical liability burden. This defensive medicine practice is also more time consuming and creates longer wait times in the emergency room. This increases dissatisfaction and raises the chances of triggering a lawsuit. Therefore, time management is a perpetual challenge for the emergency physician to maintain a balance in these parameters. I would estimate that an experienced emergency physician could reduce his number of tests by 50% if there was a much reduced liability threat. However, this defensive practice also creates a more thorough documentation trail for a physician should litigation arise.

Chapter 4

DOCUMENTATION

Documentation is important for good medical records on a patient but has become essential in a high litigation environment because lawyers would have a jury believe, as a matter of principle, that if it wasn't documented it wasn't done. This couldn't be further from the truth, since in most cases, it is impossible to document all that was said and done on every patient in a busy emergency room.

Documentation is a considerable expense on healthcare and is basically the paperwork. Emergency Room (ER) groups have struggled over the years attempting to have accurate and legible and now electronically searchable records for patient care. When I started we used written records of the SOAP format. This is a Subjective note which is the history, an Objective note which is the physical exam, an Assessment which is your impression or differential diagnosis, and a Plan which is your treatment. This was all handwritten and of varying quality and immediately available with the record for review by another doctor should the patient return on another doctor's shift. Much of this was difficult to read which is why many groups turned to dictated records of the same format. However, the costs here skyrocket as the hospital or ER groups had to pay for transcription preferably 24/7. Most often records were not able to be transcribed until the next day and of varying accuracy because most of the transcribers are not medically trained. Also common errors occur with similar phrases such as hyper and hypo. (Example: Hypertension and hypotension is frequently interposed and they mean the opposite.) Dictation would result in no record on the patient's chart until it is transcribed usually the next day, resulting in no record should the patient return before this, unless some additional hand written paper record was also allowed to be included. Also dictation results in triple the work because the doctor has to take some kind of notes in working up the patient, dictate this as completely as possible without getting similar cases confused in a busy ER. The doctor must either come in early for a shift and read, edit and sign these transcribed records from his previous shift or be able to pull them up at home on a computer for homework. If the record was not transcribed for some reason the doctor must then repeat this dictation process from memory, most likely, a few days later. This very onerous process was instituted to have legible records that were typewritten, even if they were inaccurate. Imagine how this can foul you up if an inaccurate record became part of a lawsuit. Another system became very popular to try and circumvent these difficulties called the "template system". This involved a series of one page checklists with supplemental notes focused on questions oriented to a patient's primary complaint. This system has the advantage of better legibility because of the checklists and fewer hand written notes and some prompting to consider additional diagnoses with similar complaints. However, this did not create a searchable record for the computer, but rather had to be scanned into the computer record as a picture. The latest federal requirements however are requiring searchable records and this I would agree is desirable for better patient record access and care, but the technology is deficient in that voice recognition software will have to be deployed for immediate confirmation and entry into the patient's record. This is not yet a proven successful technology for adaption to a busy emergency department (ED). Dictation will require immediate transcription and review for signing by the ED physicians with its attendant increase in time and costs. Staffing will have to be increased with any successful move to accurate electronic searchable records or the EDs will become even more backlogged. The fact that this is already law about to go into effect with the "Affordable Care Act" is evidence that the lawyers or administrators who write these laws do not visit or communicate with the front lines in healthcare such as the emergency departments of our hospitals.

Chapter 5

HEALTHCARE PRODUCT AND MEDICATION LIABILITY

Healthcare product and drug liability is the 4th and may be the most costly addition to healthcare costs and is also very difficult to quantify. This cost to healthcare was not even considered in the above Harvard study and most other studies that want to trivialize the impact of medical liability on our healthcare costs. However any product from dressings, to suture kits, to medications have a significant cost premium due to liability. Drugs have a significant cost added to them due to liability and federal regulation by the FDA. Virtually anything used in healthcare is significantly more costly due to liability. Advertising by pharmaceutical companies and lawyers has proliferated in the past few years and is creating a significant rise in the costs of prescription drugs. Just turn on your television in any city in the USA and witness all the promotions of prescription medicine by pharmaceutical companies directly to the lay public. This is followed immediately by ads from lawyers to initiate litigation over products and drugs used in healthcare for their adverse side effects. This is unethical to me. In fact, only 2 developed countries in the world allow this advertising of prescription medicine and that is the United States and New Zealand. Why should the American public be exposed to this constant badgering by these groups when the rest of the civilized world considers this unethical, inappropriate and unnecessary? What is the cost of all this advertising and isn't that passed on the consumer in their cost of medication? Recently there seems to be an explosion in class action suits by attorneys seeking windfalls by this combined litigation. Any business producing or supplying products or drugs to healthcare has a significant liability cost in their business and these costs are passed on to the end user, healthcare facilities.

Chapter 6

ADMINISTRATIVE RESPONSE TO HIGHER COSTS

The liability insurance, the defensive medicine practice and the product liability are the primary and ongoing drivers of accelerating healthcare costs. Yet the response to these issues is adding further to the costs by the growing hospital administrations trying to cope with this by attempting to reduce risks and comply with federal rules and to balance the budgets by cutting front line staff in the emergency departments. Almost all hospitals accept Medicare and Medicaid patients and federal funding for this. As a consequence, hospitals must comply with federal rules and regulations which are also increasing and generating increasing programs and paperwork. This is increasing the burden on hospitals while at the same time the government of this country is trying to pare back Medicare and Medicaid reimbursements. Additionally there is a growing Medicare population creating a growing cost burden on the system. The end result of this is a growing decline in health care services. We are witnessing a squeeze in emergency services like none I have seen in my 36 years of emergency practice. Emergency medical visits are increasing annually. Yet the staff on all levels is being reduced to meet hospital financial demands. The numbers of emergency clerks and medical technicians have been reduced. This is creating an increased burden on nursing in the ER, where they are now having to do unnecessary tasks such as stocking the ER, moving patients and routine vitals. At the same time they are being demanded to take on more patients per nurse. Morale has declined so much that the nurses are leaving the emergency departments in droves. Our quality of healthcare is in an inexorable decline if we can't change the liability climate in this country.

Chapter 7

INSURANCE RESPONSE TO THESE TRENDS

Insurance companies are not interested in genuine cost reduction in healthcare. They take in premiums and make pay outs in a manner that always result in a profit for the company at the public expense. They have responded to this growing cost of healthcare by paring back what they cover and by increasing premiums at the same time. This has forced individuals to pay exorbitant increases in premiums to stay covered. Businesses have resorted to having employees changed to part-time work thus removing their insurance benefit or by having the employee contribute to their premiums if they remain on full-time. The Affordable Care Act has deceitfully crippled the employer healthcare benefit to the working American public by making healthcare benefits provided by an employer taxable as income to begin in 2020. The insurance cost increase has been bad enough but the additional degradation in coverage has been nothing less than outright deceit. Insurance has evolved into PPOs, HMOs and EPOs which without going into detail means that this insurance has now reduced your access to doctors and facilities. This has also created a nightmare of complexity of billing for all healthcare facilities in that they have to learn about the coverage and rules required by all these various contracts such as gaining approval prior to medical service and procedures in order to have paid coverage. This includes all the billing and ancillary staff required to analyze and negotiate the complex healthcare insurance strategies and contracts now in place. I believe these policies and programs were devised to deceive the public by disguising the actual insurance coverage being offered. Just think of all the additional personnel in billing departments in all the hospitals just to deal with this complex aspect of our healthcare delivery. The insurance companies have now also introduced varying co-pays and varying deductibles and combining this with in network rates to out of network rates. These deductibles also are per family member or combined and vary with whether the deductible applies to varying situations or procedures or facilities. Deductibles also renew annually. So if you have a $5000 deductible and you have used $3000 during your policy year this will jump back up to $5000 as your next policy year starts. The same deception now exists with prescription coverage. They have established categories of coverage that are totally nebulous as far as what you will have to pay for your prescriptions until you use it. The insurance companies have all the actuarial stats on what conditions you are likely to develop in making up these policies. Now if you can compare healthcare insurance policies and think you know what you have, you are better than I. I have been an emergency physician for decades and I haven't a clue what my financial obligations may be with my insurance policy. This is outright deceit by the insurance companies. I am convinced that anyone can be wiped out of their well-being financially by a medical condition no matter what you have for coverage in the U.S. (That is unless you are a U.S. congressmen, then you'll be covered incredibly well by the taxpayers in this country and have the added benefit of a country club healthcare facility to rehabilitate in).

Ramifications to other insurances by rising medical care costs are also unrecognized by those that are giving low estimates of our healthcare costs due to liability. Besides the additional liability of adverse events of owning a car, a boat, a plane or your home, the medical costs of accidents or injuries related to these entities has given rise to all of the insurance premiums for the medical treatments under these insurances. In fact, in Michigan the greatest cost increases in auto insurance is due to the medical care coverage. Therefore, almost all of our non-healthcare insurance premiums are also rising due to the accelerating cost of medical care in America.

Hopefully, I have established how dire our healthcare prospects are from the above (I am sure most people were already aware of much of this). I am convinced that healthcare has been hijacked by the legal system in this country and I will demonstrate this in the coming chapters. I don't have the actual statistics of this monetary drain on our medical care system in America and I doubt that anyone else has this information other than major law firms. I would surmise that hundreds of billions of dollars are being siphoned out of healthcare and much of that directly into law firms from these processes due to the above medical liability issues.

These lawsuits that are being triggered by attorney advertisements and contingency fee structures are a growing burden on everyone involved except the attorneys. Even if a suit was generated by a legitimate complaining victim of deficient medical care, the legal process is totally inappropriate for all parties involved except the lawyers. This is not surprising since they and their lawyer legislator colleagues have created the laws. This, by the way, is the reason little has changed in my 36 years of practice in terms of liability reform.

Chapter 8

THE ANATOMY OF A MALPRACTICE SUIT

The initiation of a lawsuit against a doctor is an immediate loss for the doctor, even if he eventually wins his case because of the system structure. Once a doctor receives notice of a suit he (refers to he/she subsequently) must contact his attorney for his insurance and go into a mode of silence, talking to no one except his insurance attorney, whereby information that he offers is privileged and not accessible by the plaintiff attorney. If the doctor talks to colleagues or anyone, he may have to say under oath what he said to them or they may be subpoenaed to testify in this case revealing what the doctor said. This isolates the doctor, being unable to readily talk to others about this difficulty and personal distraction from his current work that may drag on for years. Next begins the discovery process in which the insurance companies find doctors of the same training as the defendant doctor and various specialty experts related to the issues in the case. These doctors review this case and the medical records and render opinions. The plaintiff attorney, even before the suit began, had to find a same specialty trained doctor as the defendant to render an opinion that indicates 3 elements: a breach in the standard of care of the patient, an injury had occurred to the patient in this care, and that the breach caused or contributed to the injury. Now this may sound somewhat challenging to a lay person if there was no actual breach in the standard of care. However, the attorneys have developed a circuit of client doctors who are paid to review and find some avenue to claim breach of standard of care. Medicine has so many grey areas that one doctor can claim a breach and that he would have done something different, especially since they are reviewing the case retrospectively. There are even several web sites now where doctors can offer their review services to the attorneys for pay. The rise in the availability of doctors to participate in this legal process is commensurate with the growing doctor dissatisfaction with the deteriorating conditions in medical care. Many doctors are looking for other sources of income outside of the actual practice of medicine. The legal review of medical cases is lucrative to these practitioners even though I believe they are contributing to the rising cost and deteriorating conditions in healthcare delivery in America. So there is no shortage of available doctors to testify against other doctors, even in this liability climate causing our healthcare demise.

Next the discovery process begins with the initiation of a lawsuit. This process of obtaining information about the case may take years to the dismay of a plaintiff injured patient and also to the defendant doctor. This process is very cumbersome, tedious, time consuming and is very expensive to the defense. They have to build a strong defensive case and this involves depositions and training for depositions by the attorneys. Many depositions are from experts from out of state. Surprisingly, no one attorney is after the truth in these cases. They are out to win a jury decision in their favor. Often they are trying to trap a defendant physician in a statement or phrase that will distort what really happened. They have all developed techniques over the years to manipulate what you say or intend to say and the rules of engagement favor the prosecution. Anything that you say in deposition can be pulled out of context and projected on a screen for the jury in court. Therefore, the defense attorneys coach the defendant doctor to say the very minimum in his deposition even though he might want to strongly expound on the subject and destroy the plaintiff case. This, however, would allow the plaintiff attorney to go back with his expert and find any avenue of weakness to exploit in court if it comes to that. This process encourages the case to drag on before eventually going to court, especially in one that is very defensible.

Later in this process, however, efforts will begin to encourage settlement. Settlement is desired by all especially the plaintiff attorneys, because they and their client get paid and the process ends. The plaintiff is anxious to get paid and end this time consuming process. The defendant doctor most often would like to know his damages are covered by his insurance. Ending the process may be less costly than considering risking the unknowns in court and the time involved. The unknowns are scary because the awards can be against the defendant doctor by a sympathetic jury for someone who has been injured, even if it wasn't the defendant doctor's fault. This may even exceed the defendant's insurance coverage for which he will be personally responsible. However, settlements encourage attorneys to bring additional contingency suits. If the case does proceed to court, the cards are stacked against the defense. First of all, the doctor will not have a jury of his peers. These will not be experienced emergency physicians to judge his case. Next he will have to abide by the rules of evidence in court. He will have to use the medical records, depositions and medical experts to make his case in court. He will not be able to lecture the jury to help them understand the issues regarding his case, complicated as they may be. He will only be able to answer questions by the plaintiff attorney and his own attorney, neither of whom may be medically trained and who are only trying to win over the jury, not trying to determine the truth. The plaintiff attorney, if the case is going poorly, may ask many irrelevant questions simply to confuse the jury especially on technical issues. The defense attorney needs to be able to counter this with his questions but can't consult with his defendant doctor on the stand to help rectify the confusion. The jury may simply decide that the doctor is rich and insured and the plaintiff is injured and deserves to have some compensation. That is not an encouraging picture for a doctor that has been dragged over the coals already before going into court even if he knows he should win. That is also what has encouraged settlement after settlement and fostered more and more litigation in our American legal system. Our court system for technical issues such as medical-legal is totally inappropriate and costly.

Chapter 9

SOLUTION

End this nonsense. Why not streamline the process? Take these issues out of the court system altogether. Eliminate the expensive lawyer middlemen from the process. Establish county boards of 3 to 5 physicians to review cases that patients present as wrongdoing and give the board the authority to make awards or dismissals of cases presented to them. Allow them as an odd numbered group to decide by majority if the 3 elements of malpractice exist. Give them the authority to demand of those doctors guilty of malpractice, remedial training or restricted practice until retrained. This would improve healthcare unlike the current system that invokes no penalty other than financial and just drives up healthcare costs. The lawyers will argue that this is like letting the wolf guard the chicken coup. I will demonstrate that this is nonsense since the current court system already requires an equally trained doctor to review the medical records and create the case for the plaintiff attorney as a matter of procedure. How biased are these plaintiff physician reviewers that are being paid thousands of dollars for their opinions on the case? Why should the doctors have to train the attorneys, judges and lay jurors about the complex medical issues to determine if there was a breach in the standard of care? The current system is more like a giant goose laying golden eggs for the unnecessary lawyers and judges, if you want to make an animal analogy. A board of laypersons with physician advisors could also oversee the system to assure that there is no collusion among the physicians. The process could all be carried out remotely over the Internet via web meetings to prevent local physicians from having to review colleague cases locally. Medical product and procedure liability should also be funneled through this county health court system and circumvent all these class action suits. How can drug companies even be sued for products that have been approved by the tedious FDA approval process for identified adverse effects as a known risk for treating a medical condition? As an example, all of our anticoagulant drugs have had class action suits for adverse bleeding events, yet they were designed to prevent clots in those patients with clotting disorders to prevent strokes and blood clots in legs and lungs and elsewhere with the known side effect of bleeding in a small percentage of patients. These drugs were all approved by the FDA for that purpose. Because it is a very complex issue deciding whether the very serious risk of these clots outweighs the serious risk of bleeding, lawyers are exploiting these adverse reactions by bringing class action suits. The lawyers could just a easily bring class action suits for those patients that suffered a stroke and had some condition that justified their doctor placing them on an anticoagulant but failed to do so because of the risk of bleeding. This and thousands of other issues in medicine present a damned if you do and damned if you don't scenario for a doctor. If the drug in question were judged to be inappropriately prescribed by a county health court or compensation board of specialists, they would appropriately deal with this as a medical malpractice event. This is another example of where a panel of experts in medicine, not lawyers, judges and/or a lay jury should be deciding whether the use of these drugs was appropriate in any given patient that had an adverse reaction.

To have any hope of reducing healthcare costs or even containing this, we have to make some dramatic changes in what is happening in healthcare today. This plan makes perfect sense and if implemented would extract the courts from the tedious time consuming inappropriate court process, at the very least, to say nothing of the healthcare cost savings.

My initial plan was to bring this to the national congress. However, I suspect that some or many states may resist a national mandate (even if that were possible) and legally reject this. I then realized that if I could convince one state to do this, that state would experience a dramatic reduction the complex costly court process. That state would see a disappearance of medical malpractice insurance premiums that could be diverted to the county health court operations. This would expedite legitimate awards for patients victimized by substandard care and improve quality by requiring remedial training to deficient doctors. A database registry could be established through this multicounty court system that would identify adverse practice patterns, adverse procedure effects and adverse drug reactions and provide an additional expedited process of notification to our healthcare providers. That state would be attractive for doctors, and eventually become a haven for businesses because of the reduced healthcare premiums. This would also become a state with a few remaining ethical attorneys as all the advertising ambulance chasing attorneys would be moving out of state. I am certain that this model would become the envy of surrounding states and eventually spread nationally.

I was hoping to bring this plan to Michigan. We could become a low healthcare cost state. We would retain our physicians trained here and have physicians moving here instead of leaving Michigan. We may even soon have a return of rural physicians and even obstetrics coverage in rural areas. Specialists would return to ER coverage. Businesses would be attracted to Michigan because of the low liability and low healthcare cost plans that could be simplified and provided to their employees. We would also unclog our court system by removing these complicated time consuming cases.

A trial study program could be initiated in a few counties evaluating malpractice cases to compare the costs and results in a blinded comparison of the current system vs. a county board system that would rule on the same cases. My efforts have fallen on deaf ears in Michigan and I continue to be totally frustrated in my efforts to pursue this as of 2015.

Politicians are confronted by rising health care costs and its impact on businesses and the economy, yet I hear no one seriously considering reducing the number one cause of escalating costs in our health care system: liability. In fact, a number of studies including the Harvard study that I used for some of the malpractice and defensive medicine stats claim that the cost savings would be only a few percent of our overall healthcare costs. The above issues that they and other studies do not address make these evaluations ridiculously inaccurate. I personally could practice doing one half the tests and procedures that I do in emergency medicine without the liability onus over my head. I would be providing better quality of care by not doing unnecessary tests, procedures and referrals to specialists and would have expedited time management (reduced wait times) in the ER. I would only be giving up this added documentation that I claim is mostly for liability protection. Now if we only cut our tests etc. by one third and reduced product liability almost completely (something that is almost completely ignored), our costs for healthcare would drop significantly. This may possibly drop our healthcare costs to a level commensurate with other developed European countries. They spend only one half of what we spend on their medical care on a per person basis. That would be a savings of hundreds of billions of dollars, a significant portion of our healthcare costs. Another onus eliminated would be a portion of the administrative and legal departments of our hospitals attempting to comply with federal programs to reduce liability risks. Additionally we need to revamp our medical insurance programs to be simplified, understandable and user friendly. This would eliminate a behemoth staff of administrators in billing departments of all healthcare facilities trying to understand and negotiate and manage medical insurance contracts. Now process that across America and you will witness a tremendous additional reduction in healthcare costs. All this aside, I will demonstrate how medical liability is not only causing healthcare costs to spiral out of control, but is in the process of ruining our quality healthcare, as I will demonstrate in the coming chapters. That is the most serious of issues related to reducing medical liability.

Chapter 10

SAMPLE EFFECTS OF MALPRACTICE LITIGATION ON ME

I am going to start by elaborating on the malpractice litigation affecting me in my 36 years of practicing emergency medicine.

I have had four cases of malpractice on me personally and one on an ER Corporation in which I was a partner in my career of full time emergency medicine practice. I am board certified in emergency medicine and recertified every 10 years since 1987. I have been an assistant clinical professor teaching clerks, interns, and residents in emergency medicine most of my career. I am a fellow of the American College of Emergency Physicians.

The Destruction of an ER Corporation by Medical Malpractice Liability

First, I will discuss the corporation suit that I did not learn about till the trial results were in because of the secrecy rule in a lawsuit cited previously in chapter 8. This case involved a 30 year old male that came to the hospital ER from work with the complaint of scapula pain. He was referred to the fast track of the ER because nursing triage felt he was a minor injury. The Physician's Assistant saw the patient and gave him a muscle relaxant and he was better and sent home. He died 8 hours later and on post mortem exam was found to have had a heart attack. The hospital, the PA, the supervising physician, and the ER Corporation were all named in a lawsuit for wrongful death. This brings me to another discussion of deep pockets. The lawyers are not concerned with whom was primarily at fault, they want to sue everyone possibly involved in the plaintiff's care, especially those with money resources. No reasonable physician felt this was a case of malpractice. There was no breach of standard of care and no causation related to that care. No one of our corporation physicians would have even ordered an EKG with this 30 year old having muscular back pain that had improved in the ER. Even if they did the EKG at this time it most likely would have been normal. Nevertheless, this patient had a bad outcome and to make matters worse he was married with 2 small children. The physicians in our corporation had $300/$600 thousand malpractice coverage at this time meaning the targeted physician only had $300,000 protection for this incident by his insurance. This physician, who was also the director of the emergency department, and the ER Corporation became the primary targets of this suit for wrongful death as the hospital managed to settle for $25,000. The physician assistant (PA) was also essentially dropped from the case because he had few resources. Considering what I said earlier about a sympathetic jury, the corporate officers and the targeted physician offered to settle for the $300,000 insurance limit. The plaintiff wife of this patient accepted. The defendant doctor's own insurance company, however, refused to settle feeling strongly that there was no malpractice and wanted to proceed to trial. Here is another onerous arrangement with our malpractice insurance providers. In the small print of our insurance policies we are required to fully participate in the insurance company's defense or we are not covered. Therefore, the physician and corporation would have to pay the $300,000 out of pocket or proceed to trial as the insurance company wanted. The insurance company had nothing to lose by going to trial since they were only responsible for $300,000 in the settlement and if they lost in a trial and the award was higher the additional cost would pass to the defendant physician and the corporation. The insurance company was advised that they would be responsible for any additional award above the $300,000 via emails by the physician and corporation defendants and this proceeded to trial. The plaintiff prevailed and was awarded $1,200,000. The insurance company refuse to pay any amount above the $300,000 policy limit. This set off the most convoluted nightmare of lawsuits that I have ever heard about that lasted for years and I believe it is still going on. The corporation, the physician and the insurance company appealed the conviction. The judge began pushing the corporation and defendant physician to begin paying the plaintiff over and above the $300,000 that the insurance company paid as these appeals dragged on. The physician and corp. had to sue the insurance company for this additional award since the insurance company forced this case into trial against the wishes of the defendants. The ER Corporation was trying to protect the defendant physician, yet had difficulty managing payroll and being competitive with hiring new quality physicians with this million dollar obligation. This actually grew to over 1.7 million because of interest of 8.5% over the years of litigation. We had an excellent ER corporation of 11 board certified doctors in the most democratic ER Corporation that I have ever been involved in. We all equally shared the shifts including nights, weekends and holidays. We split the revenue equally based on number of hours worked. We had a great connection to residency programs to obtain additional highly qualified staff. Now with this award onus, we had difficulty hiring without telling the applicants that we were under a large obligation. We were not sure how this would conclude and it became impossible to hire good new staff, so we all had to continue working longer hours than many of us wanted. We physicians in this corporation next met as a group to discuss our options. We consulted a bankruptcy attorney to devise a plan to protect the other corporate physicians by bankrupting the corporation and giving the plaintiff the accounts receivables which would amount to about $300,000. We had a settlement hearing with all the attorneys involved. There was the corporate attorney, the defendant doctor's attorney, the bankruptcy attorney, the appellate attorney, the hospital attorneys, and the insurance company attorneys, all brought together to work out how much we could generate to pay this plaintiff. The award had grown to 1.5 million at this time. No agreement could be reached and this get together cost the ER Corporation $25,000 in attorney fees without obtaining a settlement. Next, we put together a plan to borrow a million dollars and finance this over a 10 year period to come out of our accounts receivable and we would all be taking a pay cut. We then arranged another settlement hearing and threatened to bankrupt the corporation if it were not accepted. This would force the attorneys to get what they could from the accounts receivables and the defendant doctor's assets which would have been considerably less than the million dollar package collected without effort. We were dumbfounded to see the plaintiff attorneys reject this offer and the corporation was out another $25,000 in attorney fees for this meeting. A third settlement hearing was arranged as a final get together and this again resulted in a rejection of the million dollar settlement. We corporate physicians wanted to protect the defendant physician but we couldn't continue as a group unable to hire additional help and we were all working more than we wanted to keep the ER covered. This situation had dragged on for another couple of years whereby the award had grown to 1.7 million dollars. The defendant doctor was angry as he was left as the target and had to carry all the appeals since the corporation declared bankruptcy and no longer existed. The judge allowed these plaintiff attorneys to start collecting the doctor's assets and even to begin to garnish his wages as he went to work for another hospital. This was a physician that had never even seen the patient. The suit against the insurance company was eventually won by the defendant doctor and the insurance company, however, appealed which resulted in continuation of this litigation. Fortunately, another judge ended the garnishment and attachment of this doctors assets until these appeals could be heard. To my knowledge this tragedy is still going on in the courts as of 2014. A corporation was destroyed. Excellent ER coverage for this hospital was decimated as 6 of the 11 board certified doctors left or resigned their ER careers over this. This young defendant doctor had his career ruined and he did not even actually see the patient. The hospital had to scramble to get ER coverage using a hodgepodge of locums tenens coverage. I was one of the physicians that stayed at this hospital but eventually had to leave in disgust over the deteriorating conditions in this hospital ER after this ER corporation bankruptcy disaster. That is one example of heinous "American Greed" on the part of that plaintiff and/or the plaintiff's law firm that acted in a most unprofessional and inappropriate manner.

This all occurred over a bad outcome case that most sensible physicians believe was not malpractice, but was an award decided by a non-medically trained sympathetic jury. That is also one major example why this should not be in our current court system. This system does not provide a jury of our peers and these lay jurors make decisions based on other factors not the facts.

Consider this regarding this unfortunate case. Hospital ERs are where people go when they are ill. Many are in poor health and poor physical condition. In general this is a sick population that visit our ERs across the country by the "millions" every year and is growing in numbers. Just by chance some of these patients are going to arrive and be treated for an unrelated problem and will drop dead within hours of being at the hospital ER. Would you accept liability to the extent of your personal assets for the continued well-being of this population? We unfortunately are expected to do this as emergency physicians. (See my preamble). Emergency Medicine needs a break from this liability onus. All doctors should take heed to my warning of how vulnerable you are in America's liability climate as I shall now demonstrate in my own personal malpractice experience.

My Personal Medical Malpractice Liability Cases

I had my first lawsuit occur while working at a busy community ER. I received a patient via EMS with the story that he was a psychotic alcoholic that was tearing up his motel room. The staff of the motel had called the police whereby he was given a chance to go to the hospital to be evaluated or he would go to jail. Of course he chose the ride to the hospital. He had no complaints of injury but was weak and thirsty. He was a disheveled cachectic cooperative patient. He admitted that he was a street person with no relatives that he had any contact with for years. His initial vitals were normal except for a blood pressure of 80/60 and a pulse of 100. His exam was essentially normal with no significant signs of trauma and no trunk or abdominal tenderness. I felt he was probably dehydrated and did some initial blood work and gave him some IV fluids after which his pulse game down to 80 and blood pressure up to 100/80 which I felt was probably normal for this asthenic street person. His labs came back normal except for mild anemia with a hemoglobin of 12. He had no family to contact to take him home and I managed to admit him for observation and continued IV hydration to the family practice physician on call. He was admitted to the floor and 10 hour later had a seizure and died. On post mortem exam he was found to have a ruptured spleen as the cause of death. He probably had a stable ruptured spleen when I saw him and had a withdrawal seizure from alcohol in the hospital which disrupted a clot on the spleen and caused his death or it may have been SUDEP Sudden Unexplained Death in Epilepsy. Nonetheless, a lawsuit was filed against me for wrongful death and failure to diagnose a ruptured spleen. This was brought by the divorced wife of this patient who previously wanted nothing to do with him for years. I strongly felt there was no breach in standard of care and wanted to go to court, however my ER Corporation insisted I settle this case and not risk a large award due to a death of a patient. I settled for $60,000. The corporation felt that was a cost of doing business. I felt like this was feeding the sharks. Considering what happened in the above described corporation case which actually occurred many years later than my case for this same corporation, I since realized they made the most appropriate decision.

My next lawsuit came when I was working a very busy day in a busy emergency room. There was a 29 year old patient that arrived with chest pain that hurt when she breathed or moved according to a nurse that notified me, as I was busy working up and writing orders for a stroke patient. I was able to see this young patient 30 minutes after she arrived and she looked uncomfortable. As part of her workup I ordered an EKG. This was before EKGs were ordered immediately by triage nurses for anyone with chest discomfort or difficulty breathing. When I was handed her EKG I was shocked. She appeared to be having an acute anterior MI (heart attack). Luckily the cardiologist was in the ER at the time and took over her care immediately. However, our hospital did not have angioplasty available and transfer to the heart surgery hospital was hastily arranged by the cardiologist. The patient had a blockage removed by angioplasty but suffered some heart damage. A lawsuit was initiated by the patient against me, the cardiologist, the corporation and the hospital for delay in treatment. I had never before seen any female under age 30 that wasn't abusing cocaine or other stimulants have a heart attack. I settled for $30,000 in this case.

My next case was another Physician Assistant incident for which I had signed the chart as the supervising physician but I hadn't been consulted nor even seen the patient on this ER visit. This was a case of a 29 year old drug abusing migraine seizure patient that was seen by the PA after she was directed to the fast track by triage for a pain shot for chronic migraines. The patient had the same type headache that she has frequently and has had no relief with specific migraine meds and has adverse reactions to all other pain meds except narcotics. She over time has built a tolerance to narcotics and knows her dosage is higher than normal and tells the PA the dose that she needs IV (intravenous). He refuses to give her an IV and medicates her with this higher same dose by IM (intramuscular) shot. This, however, was a proper dose for a narcotic tolerant patient. She is up immediately in the hall demanding to leave with her boyfriend that brought her but now has to leave. She is released, given no prescriptions and is to follow up with a primary doctor and a pain clinic. The patient went home, the boyfriend went to work 6 hours later. She was last seen by him eating and playing on a computer 6 hours after the ER visit. The boyfriend's mother was home with the patient. The patient then went to bed and was found by the boyfriend's mother unresponsive 2 hours later. EMS was called and found the patient not breathing. They resuscitated her and transferred her to the hospital where she was admitted to ICU. A week later she was declared brain dead and eventually died having life support discontinued. Drug screens revealed polypharmacy (many drugs), many of which were narcotics and sedatives. The post declared her cause of death SUDEP (sudden unexplained death from epilepsy), since she had a seizure disorder and occasionally a seizure results in a patient not breathing adequately for an extended period and causes brain damage and eventual death. The patient also may have taken more sedatives and pain medicines at home and quit breathing with the same lethal consequences. After her demise the mother brought a lawsuit for wrongful death. The plaintiff attorney was able to find a doctor on the internet from Texas who gave a review that indicated a breach in the standard of care by criticizing the ER dosing of the narcotic. He said that the dose was too high and may have contributed to her death. The dose was appropriate for a narcotic tolerant person and would have worn off hours before her death. This case took several years, numerous depositions and hearings, mountains of paperwork before finally being dismissed by the judge a couple weeks before trial. The same drug Dilaudid was also given to the patient in the same dose one week before our ER visit at another hospital without any adverse effects. The drug should have worn off in 4 hours and 6 hours later she was eating and playing on her computer without ill effects. The plaintiff expert was finally discredited by admitting in deposition that he had only used Dilaudid once in his career and only uses Demerol. This must have cost the defense several hundred thousand dollars and untold stress to the target doctors as this case also traveled through this burdensome court system for 3 years. A panel of doctors would have dismissed this case in one brief hearing.

My latest and hopefully final malpractice suit was brought by a 38 year old healthy female that bumped her right thigh on a chair cleaning. She hurt the middle of her thigh, rubbed it and continued walking on it without using any ice or ace wrap and developed progressive pain overnight. She was seen in the ER by a colleague the day after the injury and had a tender area on her thigh with no break or discoloration in the skin. She had a very low grade fever at triage vitals of 100.6 with no other symptoms. She was x-ray negative and treated as a bruised thigh muscle, given ice instructions and a knee immobilizer without an ace wrap. The patient continued some mobility with the brace and alternated ice and heat and massaged in Icy-Hot on her thigh. She became much more swollen and painful the next day when I saw her. She was swollen from her knee to her groin and very tender but no wound or redness or discoloration except for a purplish streak down her right lateral thigh as though there may have been some bleeding into the thigh compartment. Her vitals in triage were normal. I considered that because of this improper initial treatment of applying heat to an acute injury that she may have caused herself considerable swelling and possibly a compartment syndrome. This is a rare condition in which swelling in a compartment of muscles cuts off the circulation to the muscles. I discussed this with the orthopedic surgeon on call and because he was not immediately available, he asked that I do compartment pressures. I did this and explained to the patient the seriousness of a compartment syndrome that could destroy her thigh muscles if untreated. The compartment pressures were 32 at 2 different sites which is elevated but not to the level requiring a mutilating procedure to lay open the entire thigh surgically based on a formula with her vitals being normal. The patient was given an ultrasound of her thigh showing no blood clot or significant hematoma. She had been given IV narcotics and was feeling better. She was given ice and a gentle ace wrap and elevation of her leg. She was offered admission for observation to be sure she did not progress to a compartment syndrome which we again advised was an emergency condition. She felt better and wanted to go home. I felt that if she had not caused a compartment syndrome in 2 days doing the wrong treatment that she should get progressively better doing the correct treatment. However, she was told to return if this should progress immediately, because she would require emergent surgery to open the thigh muscles and release the pressure lest she suffer severe muscle injury to her thigh. Eight hours later the patient went to another hospital with progressive pain and a falling blood pressure making this a compartment syndrome by the compartment pressure readings I had obtained at our hospital visit. Had she returned to our hospital she would have gone immediately to surgery. However, at the other hospital she was given a repeat workup and eventually after hundreds of tests and repeat compartment pressures she was taken to surgery the next morning. They found that she had a compartment syndrome caused by necrotizing faciitis, "the flesh eating bacteria", **spontaneously** occurring in her deep thigh muscles following this minor blunt trauma. The patient had to have her right leg amputated at the hip to save her life. How did this develop? This was an extremely rare case that should have been on the news. I did not hear about this until a year later when I received notice of intent to sue me for delay in diagnosis and treatment of this rare infection.

The plaintiff attorney was able to find several physicians to reverse engineer this case and claim negligence on my part knowing this patient's outcome.

To understand how outraged I was over the deposition testimony that was given by 3 plaintiff experts, I wrote to each of them after this case was settled condemning them for deceitful testimony. Basically, they all claimed that they would have suspected this extremely rare condition based on the patient's pain being out of proportion to her injury. All of them indicated that they would have done several invasive and aggressive procedures as early as the day after she bumped her thigh on a chair. First of all, pain is subjective and to consider this pain out of proportion the next day and begin aggressive procedures on this patient is totally inappropriate. A blunt injury to the thigh can be extremely painful and swollen in the next day or two especially if not treated with ice, ace compression and rest. In fact, she had applied heat and icy-hot to the area which would worsen the swelling following a fresh injury. Because of the significant swelling to her thigh and the significant pain I did consider a rare "injury related" condition called compartment syndrome and investigated that. For these plaintiff experts to pretend that they would start triple antibiotics and open explore this young patient's anterior thigh, as though they knew this was an infectious process, is unbelievable. This, in fact, would be malpractice for their early aggressive treatments. They would have to treat hundreds of thousands of similar injuries with triple antibiotics and surgical exploration before they would ever get a positive result of spontaneous necrotizing faciitis, if ever. Statistically they would kill 100 patients from adverse reactions to the antibiotics alone and 100s more from anesthesia and surgical exploration, let alone scarring the legs of hundreds of thousands of patients unnecessarily. This overuse of antibiotics would also create an epidemic of the resistant bacteria that they would hope to treat in this extremely rare case of spontaneous necrotizing faciitis.

I did report all three of these doctors to their respective licensing boards. The surgeon board in Washington felt they had no authority to investigate the surgeon because there was no breach in law. I told them that perjury is a breach of law and deceitful testimony is certainly a breach in moral and ethical standards. I was met with opposition to this opinion by their **attorney** manager who refused to allow me to talk with any of the medical members of the board. I had the same result with the **attorney** managers of the Massachusetts licensing board that refused to let me even talk to their medical reviewers. As of this writing the California board is still reviewing my complaint against the ER expert.

I wanted to sue these experts and I was told by my original defense attorney that I cannot sue these doctors in Michigan because they have immunity from prosecution in a deposition or trial for their testimony. I could not believe Michigan has a law like this. The plaintiff attorneys can get a doctor to testify totally inappropriately and they risk no chance of prosecution for their damages to the defendant doctor. This is tantamount to a ***license to pillage healthcare by plaintiff attorneys***.

I next tried to initiate a prosecution of these doctors for their testimony as perjury by the prosecuting attorney, whereby he indicated that he did not have jurisdiction since they were sworn and deposed in different states. He also indicated that they may not have immunity in those states depending on their state laws. I have been seriously frustrated by the lawyers in these states that I have contacted that refused to take a case like this. They indicated that the deposition testimony is a matter of opinion and would be too difficult to prosecute in a trial. If someone testifies that they would do a specific action in a case like mine and that they would be wrong statistically a million to one in treating similar symptoms, isn't that proof that they are being deceitful in their testimony? You could even audit these plaintiff doctor's records and prove that they do not do this action (specifically start triple antibiotics) in similar situations. Furthermore, if in fact you could prove that if they are doing this action, statistically, they would be committing malpractice. As I stated previously, their overaggressive treatments would be risking the creation of superbugs or adverse reactions to antibiotic and anesthesia in thousands of patients. My suspicion is that lawyers, in general, are not willing to take this kind of a personal injury case because the end result would be an inhibition of testimony in personal injury lawsuits by these physician experts, something a personal injury lawyer would not like to see. My frustration in this regard continues.

Chapter 11

GOALS

My reasons for writing these articles is to convince the public that their well-being is not being protected by the current legal system but is in effect destroying their healthcare and raising their medical premiums to unaffordable levels. I am also publishing these facts to warn the frontline emergency medicine physicians that their financial well-being is in jeopardy regardless of how skilled and responsible that they are in their practice. I believe that most of the ER doctors continue to work under these conditions out of ignorance of how vulnerable they are due to medical liability. Just review my liability cases presented earlier. Those doctors that have practiced for a number of years have to at least be aware of the deteriorating conditions, however. Our profession should not accept this status-quo. We have been frustrated for years by the inability to make meaningful liability reform because the majority of legislators are lawyers. I have witnessed no significant liability reform in my 36 year of practice in the emergency rooms across Michigan contributing PAC money to our state and national organizations. The lawyers are about to destroy the golden egg laying goose that is healthcare via medical liability in America. We, doctors, cannot even protest this treatment by demanding change by uniting and withholding care (I don't believe that would be ethical anyhow) to force change because of the blue sky laws that would put us in prison for such a protest. However, it is clear to me that conditions created by the legal structure today are restricting the public's access to care. Just go to your local ER and witness the congestion and backups in the waiting rooms. I and many others are leaving emergency medicine because of these conditions. We certainly are not encouraging our children to go into medicine because of these worsening conditions. Statistically 9 out of 10 doctors are not encouraging their children to go into healthcare. That is a tragedy and brain drain for medical care in the USA.

I did come up with an idea that does not transgress the law but will get the attention of the legislators. I propose that our state and national organizations call for a moratorium on plaintiff chart review. The plaintiff attorneys must have an emergency medicine expert review and identify a breach in standard of care by the accused doctor for a suit to proceed. This would not bring all lawsuits to a halt but would certainly inhibit many of them from going forward. I have no delusion that we will have total support among the doctors for this moratorium. A number of ER physicians will continue to support this corrupt legal structure for the thousands of dollars in blood money given to them by plaintiff attorneys. They will justify their actions as being important for the protection of the public from deficient care. That is totally wrong as I have indicated in these articles. Our licensing boards should scrutinize these plaintiff ER experts thoroughly however, and penalize them appropriately for any false or deceitful testimony. Our certification boards should also scrutinize them for ethical violations and remove their certifications if justified. We physicians are our own worst enemy in this issue and I blame us for contributing to this healthcare liability crisis. I am aware that there will be some injured patients by breach in standard of care, but they will eventually be addressed after the moratorium plays out. The overall issue of healthcare skyrocketing costs and deterioration in ER conditions dwarf this concern and in fact is contributing to breaches in healthcare standards.

Chapter 12

PHYSICAL THREAT FROM ACTUAL ADVERSE WORKING CONDITIONS IN THE ER

I am going to now depict the reality of adverse working conditions of ER shift work. Emergency medicine is in my opinion the most high risk career that anyone could choose today. When I started my career in the late 70s doing full time emergency medicine we physicians had to worry about hepatitis B and TB as a general infectious risk to our well-being as a front line medical staff. Gradually over the years we have seen the rise of hepatitis C, HIV, epidemic MRSA (Methicillin-Resistant Staph Aureus) as well as many other resistant bacteria, anthrax and now Ebola as well as many new resistant viruses. We have had rare accidental chemical or radiation disasters under normal conditions. Now we have terrorism which builds the threat of a host of intentional disasters from bioterrorism like anthrax and the plague, to chemical terrorism such as ricin and serin gas, to radiation disasters like a dirty bomb or a nuclear power plant explosion. In addition, we have all the physical traumatic consequences of terrorism from events like the trade center crashes, to school shootings from foreign and home grown terrorists. We have always had the trauma from motor vehicle crashes and injuries from domestic or community altercations to deal with in the ER. However, now the ERs have been deemed the drunk tanks of the community with all the attendant hostility from these impaired people. There is nowhere to send them until they are deemed sober or taken to jail for threatening or actually attacking the healthcare providers. The ERs are also now the community mental health stations where every mentally impaired patient must be medically evaluated by the ER doctors, whereby they can only then be transferred to a mental health facility which are frequently full or unavailable. This leaves these patients under observation for hours and days in the ER. Some have to be chemically or physically restrained to protect themselves and/or the staff from violence.

The Michigan legislature has failed to even pass legislation that would make it a felony for someone to assault a healthcare worker, as it already is a felony to assault police and rescue workers. Where do these assaultive individuals to the police and rescue workers end up? Most often they are brought to the ERs. ERs have always been a concentration of community infectious diseases like the flu for which the healthcare workers must try to protect themselves. However with the liberal travel worldwide into the United States virtually any disease in the world can wind up presenting in our ERs. I view ER personnel as the canaries of the communities. Just as the canaries of the miners warned them of bad air when the birds started dropping dead in the mines, when the ER personnel start dropping dead we may have our first warning that something bad has been released into our communities.

My personal experience with health threats have been occasional coughs in my face by careless patients, blood thrown or spattered on me before personal protection gear has been dawned in violent patients or trauma and air breathed in a non-negative pressure room when a TB patient has been later identified. I have had a few patient contaminated needle sticks over the years resulting in no known contraction of disease. In one particular case, I was sewing a known hepatitis C patient's inner thigh when he moved and bumped the curved needle coming out of his thigh into my finger through my glove drawing blood. I had to be checked over the next year with repeat blood tests and fortunately did not turn hepatitis C positive. I also had a serious encounter with a gang member that was brought in impaired by a fellow gang member within ½ hour of ingesting multiple handfuls of drugs in an overdose. When I told him he would have to have an IV and a lavage of his stomach, he threatened to come back and kill me and my family if I did any procedure on him and he cited multiple drive by shootings as part of his sordid past. I gave him an amnestic drug (causes sedation and memory loss), did the procedures and he woke up the next day and couldn't remember anything that happened. However, I obtained a gun permit to carry after this event.

Given this threat to my personal health and well-being I will next cite the medical liability threat to my financial well-being.

Chapter 13

FINANCIAL THREAT FROM ER WORKING CONDITIONS

Working in the ER, we doctors do not have an established relationship with the patients we treat. We don't know their backgrounds and personal medical histories. We must have considerable training and knowledge of all medical specialties because we may have to treat and stabilize anything from a trauma patient to a heart transplant patient that just left a tertiary hospital center. We must determine their condition and past history in an expeditious manner and render appropriate treatment. We must do annual CME to stay abreast of the escalating changes in information in all these fields. Now come the lawyers to pillage healthcare. I was told when I started ER medicine in 1977 that we only had 200/600 thousand medical malpractice liability coverage at the cost of $35,000 per year because the hospital was the deep pocket. For 20 years I never had a lawsuit and in the last 10 years I have had 3 against me, 1 against a PA that I had to sign the chart for and 1 against a corporation that I was a partner in. I was also told that the attorneys would never seek your personal assets or garnish your wages in a medical malpractice case. None of that is true based on my personal lawsuit experience. The hospitals have never remained in a united defense with my cases and always settled for $25,000 or less leaving me, the doctor, to fend for myself. See the lengthy details in previous chapter "My Personal Liability Experience". I don't believe there was malpractice in any of these cases. It is incredible to believe that there is a cesspool of scoundrel doctors in America willing to give deceitful testimony on behalf of plaintiff lawyers for a few thousand dollars in blood money. This is driving up the cost of everyone's medical care, including their own. There are actually regular conferences now being promoted to physicians to learn how to earn extra money serving lawyers in this litigation cesspool. The advertising and contingency fee structure of our legal system is unethical in other developed countries and is the driving force behind liability in this country. Working in the ER you are guaranteed to have bad outcomes regardless of how skilled and capable you are. Bad outcomes bring lawsuits and potentially disastrous financial results to the doctor, no matter how appropriate your treatment was. I will give a repeat summary of the medical malpractice cases that ruined my career in emergency medicine. I could have lost my entire estate and all of my personal assets that I had acquired over 36 years of front line emergency medicine working full time including nights, holidays and weekends on behalf of the public from any of these cases. My 1st case of malpractice liability came from the divorced wife of an alcoholic psychotic street person that died in the hospital 8 hours after stabilization in the ER following a seizure. I had only $200,000 liability coverage at the time but was forced to settle for $60,000 by the same corporation that I worked for in the previous described corporate litigation event even though I was certain there was no malpractice and wanted to go to court. The corporation knew that a wrongful death decision against me and the corporation could easily reach one million dollars by a sympathetic jury and the corporate case years later demonstrated how true that is. My second case was settled for $30,000 as I was somewhat of a 2ndary target. I had only $300,000 malpractice insurance coverage at the time and could have lost over a million dollars in a trial for a 29 year old female that suffered a heart attack and some heart damage had she won. There was no breach in standard of care in that EKGs were not automatically done by nursing triage in this era. The cardiologist also became the primary target for delay in treatment whereby she suffered some heart damage before she was able to get her angioplasty treatment. I suffered through another case that was seen by a Physician Assistant with the threat of significant personal financial loss to me. I had $300,000 malpractice coverage for this case. I did not see or consult on this patient but signed the chart for the PA under my supervision. There was no malpractice and a medical panel would have thrown this case out in a few hours of review. This case carried on to my dismay for 3 years before finally being dismissed a few days before trial in 2012. I was determined to go to trial even with a multimillion dollar award at stake for wrongful death in this 29 year old because this was clearly no breach in standard of care yet again I could have had a multimillion dollar award against me from a sympathetic jury had the case not been finally dismissed by the judge before trial by overwhelming evidence. Another case impacting me financially was the corporation case also seen by a PA, signed by another target doctor in our ER Corporation in which I was a partner. There was no malpractice but another bad outcome that resulted in the most convoluted series of lawsuits that I have ever heard of. The $1,200,000 award granted by a sympathetic lay jury resulted in the bankruptcy destruction of one of the best and only democratic ER corporations in the state of Michigan. All the doctors including me that were partners had to give up their corporation and the accounts receivables and find new less favorable financial ER contracts. Yet this was not nearly the trauma that the target doctor had to suffer. He had not even seen or been consulted on this patient, but had signed the PA chart as his supervisor and became the target for these greedy plaintiff attorneys. They attached his assets and garnished his wages until he eventually won his case against his malpractice carrier that in this situation had forced him into trial against his will when the plaintiff had actually agreed to a $300,000 settlement before trial. The destruction of this ER Corporation also ruined the ER care at this community hospital as 6 of the 11 board certified ER doctors left. The hospital had to scramble and assemble a menagerie of doctors to cover the ER. I eventually had to leave also because conditions and wait times became so adverse at this hospital. The last malpractice suit that drove me out of my medical ER practice was from an illegal immigrant. I had one million dollars malpractice coverage at this time. My insurance agency settled this case for $850,000 rather than risk a multimillion award that may be granted to this patient by a sympathetic lay jury in a trial. This was a healthy 38 year old patient that lost her leg by developing necrotizing faciitis "the flesh eating bacteria" spontaneously deep in her thigh after a minor bump to her thigh without a scratch or a mark on the outside skin. This is an extremely rare infection to occur spontaneously but has happened in cases of immunocompromised people such as patients with HIV, organ transplant patients on immunosuppressive drugs and type 1 diabetics. I searched the medical literature and couldn't find a case like this in a healthy young person in the history of medicine. I wanted to take the insurance company's settlement offer, indemnify them and go to court and personally cross examine the plaintiff experts and expose their deceitful testimony. I was unable to arrange this because of the other named doctor in this case and the insurance company's 2 million dollar exposure for the combined defense of both of us defendant doctors. Non-the-less the patient received $500,000. The attorney received $300,000 on this one case, more than I have ever made in a "year" of front line emergency medicine working full time covering nights, holidays and weekends. Of course the attorney had to receive an additional $50,000 to cover his court costs in this settlement. I was extremely upset when this settled against my will after a year of anguish in mid-2014. I would estimate that the defense spent $200,000 on this case. Therefore, a million dollars came out of healthcare over this one case in which there was no malpractice but a bad result.

The icing on the cake in this case is that this patient is an "illegal" immigrant. She would most likely have died if she had been in Mexico. I thought she was a green card immigrant throughout this case because I saw that she had $87,000 of her medical bills paid for by Medicaid. How does it happen that our tax dollars are being used to pay the medical bills of illegal immigrants? Apparently our brilliant politicians have created another benefit program for illegals at taxpayer expense. I asked my attorneys after her illegal status was determined in deposition why they did not turn her in to immigration and have her deported ending this case without this $850,000 settlement. She had her life saved and her medical expenses paid for by our taxpayers through Medicaid. The attorneys replied that (get this) it would be unethical. So, as a board certified conscientious practitioner of emergency medicine in the USA, I am required to take care of anyone that presents themselves for evaluation in our ERs including criminals. They then, however, even have the right to sue me for dissatisfied care or bad outcome and have a "**promoted opportunity**" to win my entire estate from 36 years of emergency medicine practice "**at no cost**" to them with our contingency system even if no malpractice occurred. Talk about unethical. Only in America!

I suffered Post Traumatic Stress Disorder over this case and have been unable to return to front line emergency medicine even though I am at my peak in terms of training and experience. This is evident to me by sleepless nights mulling over this case to flashbacks over the depositions and settlement discussions over this case. Fortunately writing about this has been therapeutic for me. What a waste of our medical resources! This case drove me out of emergency medical care. In retrospect, I am fortunate that I did not personally take this faciitis case to trial realizing that a sympathetic jury award in this case would have been a multimillion dollar award for this young patient for life long care. This would have wiped me out financially. Not only is this malpractice liability a financial threat but it is an emotional drain on our emergency personnel. The financial drain on healthcare itself is devastating but the adverse effects on healthcare delivery is even more important.

Chapter 14

ADVERSE EFFECTS OF MEDICAL LIABILITY ON HEALTHCARE DELIVERY

Every product and drug we use in medicine has a growing liability cost as the lawyers are flocking to class action suits over everything used in healthcare. There are frequent shortages of vaccines and common IV drugs used in the ER over liability issues that has become much more severe in the last few years. There must be billions of dollars flowing out of healthcare into law firms annually. Add to this the impact on day to day care of what is termed "defensive medicine" which are unnecessary tests, procedures and referrals that we are all doing in fear of lawsuit. We are being overwhelmed by efforts to document our care thoroughly in every patient to protect ourselves, which is increasing work load, reducing productivity and increasing wait times. The skyrocketing cost of healthcare is resulting in hospital staff reductions of clerks and techs resulting in nurses having to do more tasks such as stocking the department and carry more patients per nurse. Many nurses are leaving ER medicine for less demanding work. This is a disaster in ER delivery of incredible proportion. No ER can function to a top notch level with the depletion of this quality staff no matter how skilled the ER physicians are because these personnel are required to deliver it. Physician Assistants and Nurse Practitioners are being hired to supplement productivity. Add to this deteriorating environment by the departure of coverage in the ERs of many specialists and subspecialists. None of the ENT, plastic surgeons, hand surgeons, oral surgeons and many general surgeons want to be on call for the ERs. They recognize the hostile medical liability associated with ER medicine and have tried to avoid being on call for the ERs. The hospitals have required them to be on call or lose their hospital privileges. However, they have responded by starting surgery centers and dropping their hospital privileges, if necessary. Take note of all the surgery centers formed in the last 10 years. The end result is such a dramatic shortage of specialists at every community hospital. The care for many patients with trauma or specialty conditions is being delayed and neglected. These patients are having to be transferred to distant tertiary hospitals to find appropriate care from these specialists, a very risky road trip in many cases. Some days I have spent more time on the phone trying to arrange transfer of these patients than I did in their stabilizing care. I will cite a couple of example cases for me personally affected by this trend. Case 1: While I was working at a Michigan community hospital EMS arrived with a plumber who fell and broke a porcelain toilet severely lacerating his forearm. The EMS crew had to apply a tourniquet to control the bleeding. Upon arrival to the ER I realized that the plumber had lacerated arteries and tendons in his forearm. I could not find a vascular surgeon on call to come into this community hospital nor any hospital within 100 miles. I hastily arranged for transfer to a tertiary teaching hospital 2 hours away. I had ace wrapped his arm from fingers to forearm to squeeze the blood out of his veins and applied a blood pressure cuff for direct pressure over the wound. This obtained satisfactory control of the bleeding without tourniquet pressure. In route the bleeding increased and the EMS crew had to increase the pressure to tourniquet level. Fortunately he made it to the other hospital and into surgery before significantly damaging his hand from lack of circulation. At this community hospital we previously had ready access to hand and vascular surgeons. Another relatively common type of case are cosmetic wounds to women and children especially. Most community hospitals used to have the plastic and hand surgeons on call to come in and take these people to surgery and meticulously clean and repair their wounds under anesthesia. Now there are virtually no plastic or hand surgeons on call in most community hospitals anymore and the ER doctors are forced to patch up these people under adverse conditions in the ER and send them to the surgeon's office the next day for follow up and/or secondary revision. Many times they wind up back in the ER because the surgeon's office has an upfront charge before they can be seen and many patients can't afford this. This is not quality medical care. As you might expect these result in more lawsuits for the ER doctors. Another personal example of this is case 2. I had a 6 year old female that the parents brought to the ER having been bitten in the face by her dog. Most of the wounds were punctures but there were cosmetic wounds under her right eye and on her forehead. I called the local plastic surgeon who was not on call (because of the dropped hospital privileges working out of a surgery center) and he agreed to follow up on her the next day in the office. He asked that I clean and patch up the wounds to the best of my ability that evening. This is a challenge for any ER doctor because you have to find time to do this repair and manage all your other cases in a busy ER. The repair is very difficult under these circumstances. However since the repairs are urgent but not emergent and you may have to stop and tend to other emergent cases in your ER. Next, you have a difficult patient because of her age. You need some method of anesthesia which may be a topical or local injected anesthetic which you might imagine may not be well tolerated by a 6 year old. You may opt for moderate sedation of a child in the ER with something like Ketamine. This requires monitoring staff and gives you 30 to 45 minutes to do your cleansing and approximating the wounds. However, if other more urgent cases present to the ER you must stop your procedure and consider re-sedation later, a very risky option. I chose the former and you can imagine after giving local shots to the face of a 6 year old that I had a terrorized screaming patient to deal with. She had to be restrained by several staff to try and do this delicate procedure even though after the shots she should experience no significant pain. This is totally inappropriate and should have been taken to the OR (operating room) by a plastic surgeon to cleanse and repair under very controlled conditions. Legislation is needed now to relieve this ER liability climate for these specialists.

Chapter 15

MICHIGAN MEDICAL LIABILITY REFORM

There has been no significant medical liability reform in the 36 years that I have practiced ER medicine in Michigan. In the last few years I have witnessed the failure to pass legislation that would make assaulting a healthcare worker a felony. I have seen legislation to make ER medicine come under the gross negligence standard shot down by both defense and plaintiff attorneys, as this would have severely limited litigation for both groups of lawyers. Similar legislation to protect the subspecialists that I just depicted, to encourage them to be on call was also dismissed by the Michigan legislature. I have only seen legislation called the "I'm Sorry Law" passed that would allow a doctor to express his sympathy to an injured patient without considering that to be admitting negligence. That almost comical law is "a poke in the eye" to all medical practitioners and should demonstrate the futile nature of expecting any relief from the deteriorating conditions in the ER from our lawyer legislators.   How does our legislature find the time and need to pass such a law? I can just envision the chucklehead legislators snickering over coming up with this name for such meaningless liability reform. What was the driving force to push legislation like this to passage when they can't pass a law to make it a felony to attack and injure healthcare workers in their necessary important work rendering aid to hostile patients? Were the Hallmark lobbyists prodding them vigorously to encourage doctors to send sympathy cards to all their sick and injured patients? This is like legislating someone's thoughts. I can see the jurors now having been instructed by a Judge about this law saying in their deliberations something like this: "I don't know what all this mumbo jumbo about necrotizing faciitis means but I think he must be guilty because he sent the victim a sympathy card. Oh, but we have to ignore that in our decision". Yes, I believe these jurors will be bound by that as much as I believe Santa comes down everyone's chimney on Christmas. This legislation should make it clear that even the legislators are convinced that the jurors are making decisions in these complex medical cases not from the medical facts but from some emotional factors by which they somehow think they can legislate control. I hate my taxes when I think that these legislators are being paid by me to make laws like this. Furthermore, my effort to chastise the plaintiff experts for their deceitful testimony in depositions in my last case made me realize that these Michigan legislators created a law that provides immunity from prosecution for any doctor testifying in a deposition or trial. These plaintiff experts now can safely say anything to support litigation against another doctor even if it is deceitful. Once again I claim that this virtually gives attorneys ***a license to pillage healthcare in Michigan***. For the salvation of our emergency medical care something dramatic has to be done.

Chapter 16

THE PUBLIC'S ROLE

The public has an important role to play in this crisis. We must stop this insane litigation explosion. No one can watch television and not be overwhelmed by the lawyer's liability promotions. Nearly every medical product that is advertised has an ad by lawyers calling for a class action lawsuit against that product immediately following the promotion and side effect cautions by the medical company. The public must recognize this and protest the escalation in their medical premiums as a direct result of this liability. We should have never allowed advertising of prescription medications and ads by professionals in this country. We certainly should not have allowed contingency fees for lawsuits. Both of these issues are considered unethical in other developed countries. Class action suits are even illegal in other developed European countries. These developed countries do not seem to be impaired by this. In fact, I would suggest that this has maintained a high professional doctor-patient relationship based on trust which has been destroyed in our litigious healthcare system. No wonder our healthcare does not compare in cost to the rest of the developed world. No other country has the liability onus that is ubiquitous in America. In this national election year the public has not one politician supporting dramatic change to medical liability and I believe that this is the only solution to the healthcare cost crisis. We need to confront and question our legislators and politicians on these issues until we generate a movement to change the status quo.

The current system is so embedded in our society that I believe it has actually changed our moral standards. We have been taught as a generation has grown up with the news and advertisements by lawyers that we are not responsible for anything that goes wrong and somehow someone else or some company must be at fault. The media itself has become party to this deterioration in our self-responsibility by the overwhelming attorney advertisements and pharmaceutical ads as well as the news hype over litigation issues that fill the news these days. I wonder how much money the media gets from law firms and pharmaceutical companies for ads each year. In addition does it not surprise people that immediately after an ad from a pharmaceutical company for a medication that an ad for class action suits comes up for the adverse side effects of that drug? Do you think there may be collusion between the media and law firms to structure this? Finally, does the media really want to see this change to no ads on television for these liability issues? The number of lawyers is also escalating as they create work for themselves by leaching off all businesses and professions. I am amazed that the lawyers themselves are not restricting their numbers by higher standards and limitation of law schools. Instead they have created open enrollment law schools with liberal admission requirements flooding our society with more lawyers. I contend that lawyers, in general, are a drain on our system. They are generally non-productive. They leach off of all businesses, professions, and individuals. They and their legislative partners complicate the world with more complex laws and rules that sustain work for themselves. What does that portend for the future of American society?

I hope we haven't reached the point of no return. I have been extremely frustrated writing about these issues to the governor of Michigan and the media. I've taken up this cause because I am concerned for our future healthcare as a nation and especially for my children and grandchildren. I could uproot and move to another country with decent healthcare and lower cost of living as an easy alternative to fighting this overwhelming uphill battle to save healthcare in America, yet I would be abandoning my principles and my family who will suffer the consequences if we continue down this unsustainable road with our current system.

Hopefully I can persuade the emergency medicine state and national organizations to call for this moratorium on plaintiff chart review and get the cooperation of our legislators to realize the dire direction that we are headed to if healthcare liability doesn't change dramatically. I want to see county healthcare courts or compensation boards setup and staffed by ER physicians to determine breach of standards of care in the ERs and make appropriate awards expeditiously and make appropriate remedial training to the breaching physician if necessary. This system would protect the public from poor standards of care, improve healthcare delivery, expedite plaintiff issues in a very timely manner, unburden our current court system and put an end to these unethical class action suits against FDA approved drugs and procedures. This will reduce healthcare costs immensely. A system like this I have said could be handled over the internet by physicians in different counties to avoid interaction with cases against friends and colleagues and an ombudsman committee could be established to review cases and oversee that there is no collusion among physicians. A system like this would allow all the malpractice premiums to be collected in a massive fund that would serve to pay awards to the appropriate injured plaintiff patients and the costs of operating the county healthcare court system. The healthcare cost savings would be incredible compared to our current court and insurance costs. A brief study could be conducted to prove this but a simple analysis of what went into my malpractice cases alone should make it clear that the cost savings would be immense. Additional benefits would be that ER physicians would have a burden lifted from their shoulders in that any complaint would be evaluated by a committee of their peers and not having the lay public making awards based on non-medical factors. I can envision this eventually reducing the defensive medicine practice by ER physicians under this system for a dramatic additional medical care cost savings in America and streamline the delivery of emergency care. This would also reduce the adversarial climate between physician and patient that is promoted under our current system.

The benefit to the public should be a significant reduction in medical premiums in states where this system is in place with improved medical coverage and improved ER staffing and healthcare delivery.

The adverse impact will be the loss of liability work for attorneys both plaintiff and defense attorneys, the loss of television ads for liability issues to the television networks, and the removal of liability insurance carriers from this medical malpractice venue.

In time, a health court low cost healthcare system may finally reverse the deceitful tactics of the insurance companies to begin clearly defined benefits, simplify billing statements and rid themselves of large deductibles, co-pays and network qualifications for payments of medical care. The reason I focus on emergency medicine to initiate these changes in our liability coverage is that I have had a long career of full time emergency medicine experience to witness what is happening in emergency medicine delivery. Emergency medicine is also unique in that it is the front line in healthcare delivery. Emergency medicine incorporates front line protection and treatment for primary care, all specialties and subspecialties requiring broad based knowledge in an ever changing world of advancing information. The public generally has no relationship to the ER doctors as they do to a primary care physician and must rely on the expertise of these highly trained rigorously tested professionals. The ER doctors in this country are also the canaries of the medical community getting first exposure to all the infectious diseases (HIV, TB, and Hepatitis etc.) and chemical disasters in the community including those caused by terrorism. This is a high risk profession. Should not their care be more appropriately judged by a panel of similarly trained professionals? Should they not be protected from a liability case that could take all their personal assets even if there was an error in the work that they do?

The lawyers in this country created this disaster and they should not be surprised at the consequences of their overindulgence in medical liability. I cannot believe that they do not realize that they are killing the golden egg laying goose by pillaging healthcare with their relentless liability attacks on everything and everyone involved in healthcare. Are they not aware of the premium increases in medical care for themselves and their families? Are they not aware of the declining deceptive medical insurance coverage that they are receiving? Are they not aware of the declining staffs in the ERs and increasing wait times across this country? Are they not aware that they have created an adversarial position between the doctor and his patients?

The politician lawyers and the president have completely ignored liability in trying to address the accelerating cost of medical care in America. The affordable healthcare act is the solution that they have come up with. Do they really believe Obamacare is reducing healthcare costs? The creators of this program are corrupt in that they deceived the public in promoting this as a cost reduction plan when this does nothing to reduce costs but simply shifts the costs to our younger healthier population by forcing them to pay for health insurance. Obamacare is like a huge Medicaid program that will transfer the costs to a healthy young population for all those that formerly could not afford medical insurance premiums. This is a new financial burden primarily on our younger population. This program will now cause a surge in ER visits with low reimbursement or many unpaid ER bills to a much larger population because the primary care physicians will not see these patients just as they refuse to take Medicaid patients because of its poor reimbursement. That is a looming disaster for everyone as the ER wait times will accelerate, patient dissatisfaction will surge and the ER doctors will experience a rise in liability as they try to time manage this dissatisfied population.

The general population must start a campaign to "Get Healthcare Out of the General Court System". They must confront these issues and realize that there is no other solution to reduce healthcare costs than to reduce liability issues in our society. I know this is an uphill battle because of the incredibly large lawyer population in America. Everyone has a lawyer friend and many of the population have a lawyer in their family. Yet this is the profession that is responsible for accelerating healthcare costs and must be the profession that takes a pay cut. The role that lawyers play in healthcare is not beneficial to anyone in the population except the lawyers themselves. As I have pointed out, a health court structure or compensation board would eliminate their role in medicine and provide us with a dramatic cost savings in healthcare. Too bad for us that the lawyer legislators make the rules. That is what has gotten us in this unsustainable rising cost of medical care in the first place.

I am calling for the general population to demand changes in our liability laws to unburden our medical caregivers. Call your legislators and demand dramatic change. Ask them to establish a health court or compensation board structure and eliminate the quagmire of our current court system and the waste of time and money associated with this system. Ask them to eliminate professional advertising and eliminate contingency fees. I am going to call for a moratorium on plaintiff chart review by all ER doctors and maybe the legislators will find some incentive to act on society's behalf and not the lawyers' behalf.

The American Bar Association is the most powerful lobby In America. Even though the issues that I have addressed should make it clear that what I am proposing are the appropriate actions for saving our emergency medical care, the ABA will oppose them vigorously.

No one should have to work under these risky threatening conditions least of all the critically important emergency medicine personnel that we are all dependent on for skilled front line healthcare.

This should make it clear why most doctors are not encouraging their children to go into healthcare. We ER doctors are all witnessing this deterioration in ER working conditions without hope for some resolution in sight.

As my preamble to this book says: *"Would you enter a career that makes you personally responsible for the well-being of priceless items (humans) whose natural course is deterioration and death to the extent that this career responsibility threatens the loss of all of your own personal assets from medical liability and this career environment significantly threatens your own health and well-being?*

That is the sacrifice that one **must** accept today to enter a physician career in frontline emergency medicine!

THAT IS UNACCEPABLE AND MUST CHANGE!

Chapter 17

MY WISH LIST

I am calling for a moratorium on plaintiff chart reviews

I am appealing to **ALL PHYSICIANS** to stop doing plaintiff chart reviews. We alone can stop this carnage to our healthcare and force the creation of a county health court system if we unite and stop participating in the current medical liability system. Those plaintiffs affected by this can be addressed in the county health court when the moratorium plays out. End the adversarial relationship between us doctors and our patients that is promoted in the current system.

Following is my list of necessary changes for the public to demand from our legislators:

Get healthcare out of the current court system, which is inappropriate.

Establish county health courts or compensation boards.

Eliminate professional advertising, which is unethical.

Eliminate prescription drug advertising, which is unethical.

Eliminate contingency fee structure for lawyers, which is unethical.

Eliminate class action suits, which are unethical.

Eliminate FDA approved product suits, which are inappropriate.

Reduce the number of lawyers, by having higher admission standards not open enrollment law schools.

Simplify health insurance policies.

Simplify and eliminate many of our laws in general as a "productive" task for lawyers and legislators in America.